Eileen Carney Hulme

*With best wishes
Eileen.*

The Stone Messenger

Indigo Dreams Publishing

First Edition: The Stone Messenger
First published in Great Britain in 2015 by:
Indigo Dreams Publishing
24, Forest Houses
Cookworthy Moor
Halwill
Beaworthy
Devon
EX21 5UU

www.indigodreams.co.uk

Eileen Carney Hulme has asserted her right under the Copyright, Designs and Patents Act 1988 to be identified as the author of this work.
©2015

ISBN 978-1-909357-86-0

British Library Cataloguing in Publication Data. A CIP record for this book can be obtained from the British Library.
This book is sold subject to the condition that it shall not, by way of trade or otherwise, be lent, re-sold, hired out, or otherwise circulated without the author's and publisher's prior consent in any form of binding or cover other than that in which it is published and without a similar condition including this condition being imposed on the subsequent purchaser.

Designed and typeset in Palatino Linotype by Indigo Dreams.
Cover design by Ronnie Goodyer at Indigo Dreams

Printed and bound in Great Britain by 4edge Ltd.
www.4edge.co.uk

Papers used by Indigo Dreams are recyclable products made from wood grown in sustainable forests following the guidance of the Forest Stewardship Council.

In memory of John and Mary Carney

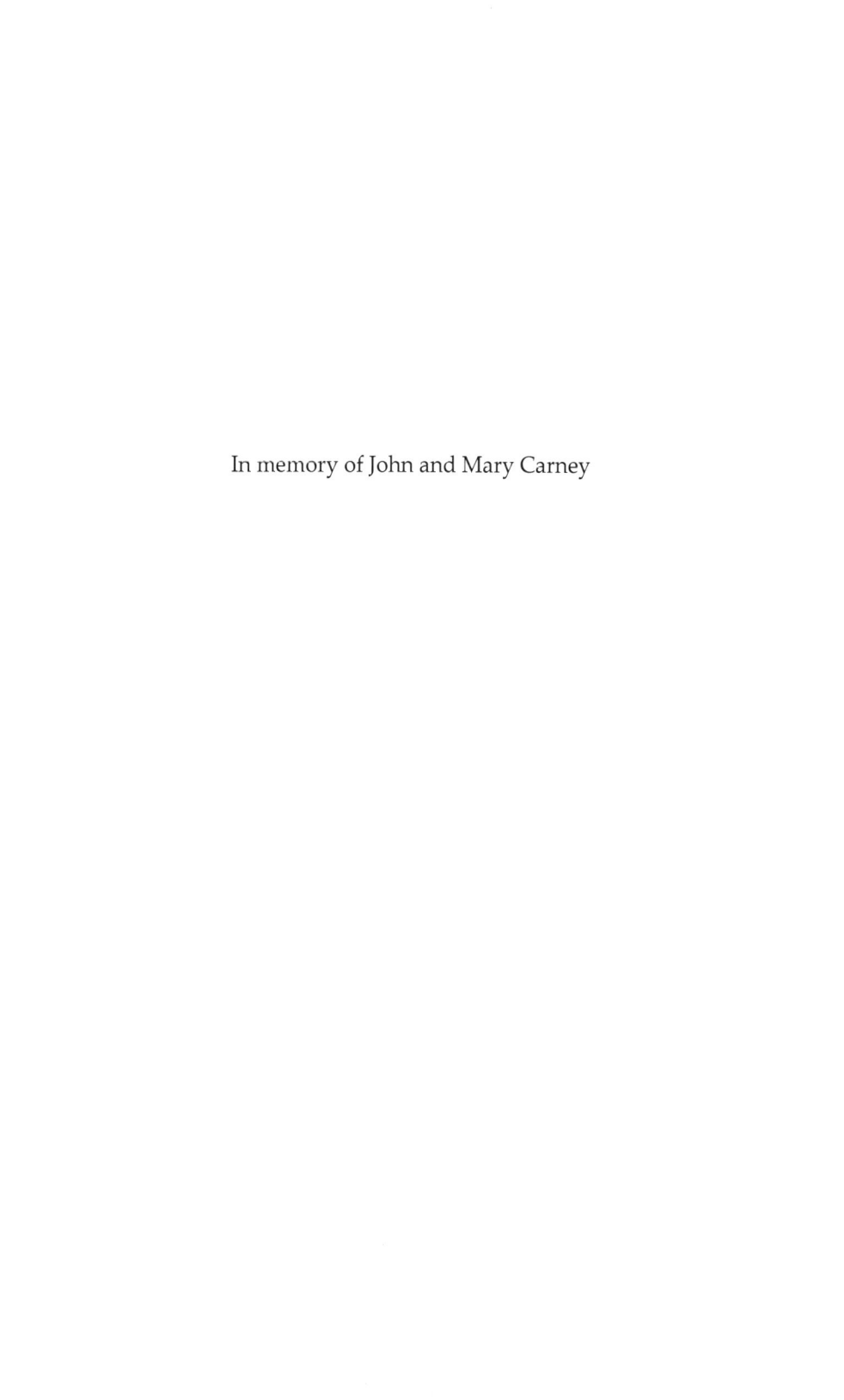

Acknowledgements

I am grateful to the editors of the following poetry magazines, journals, anthologies and internet poetry places in which poems since my last collection and poems in this collection have appeared: Acumen, Aspire, Drey, Envoi, Ink Sweat and Tears, Northwords Now, The Poetry Kit's Caught in the Net, Orizont Literar Contemporan Bucharest, Poetry Space, Purple Patch, Reach Poetry, Sarasvati, Sentinel Literary Quarterly, The Dawntreader, The Federation of Writers Scotland Anthology, The Open Mouse, The Poetry Locksmith USA, The Scottish Association of Writers. Special mention to my wonderful publishers Ronnie Goodyer and Dawn Bauling for all things writerly, and deepest gratitude to Ronnie for accompanying me on my poetry journey since the first collection. I am enormously grateful to Richie McCaffery for his close reading of the poems and his invaluable suggestions.

Other publications by Eileen Carney Hulme

The Space Between Rain, 2010, IDP.
Stroking The Air, 2005, Bluechrome.

CONTENTS

This is how it was 9
Navigate by Moonlight 10
For My Birthday 11
Guilt is Quiet 12
Thinking of my Mother as Lauren Bacall 13
The Kindling 14
Looking at Jane Morris 15
The way I learned to tell the time 16
The Master Butcher 17
Winter 1960 18
Leaving the Funeral Home in Enniskillen 19
January 20
Blue Monday 21
Walking Through the Door 22
Blue for Best 23
The Box at the bottom of the Wardrobe 24
Lowering the Coffin 25
Handle with Care 26
Stele 27
Clearing the Path 28
Coping Stones 29
Walking with Ghosts 30
With a Feather in your Hat 31
Thoughts of Spring 32
Scotland to Sarajevo 33
Mushrooms 34
Sarajevo Springtime 35
Sarajevo to Dubrovnik 36
From the great book of distances 37
The Way of Tea 38

Breaking Bread 39
The Breathing Space 40
Finding Blue.. 41
If We Choose To Speak... 42
When I am Not 43
Over Time 44
When Buttons Surprise 45
In a World of Positives 46
You Were Summer.. 47
After all this time... 48
Returning to where I've always been............................ 49
The Stone Messenger 50
Findhorn holds my breath 51
Blue Hour 52
Seen in my everyday 53
How It Was 54
Resident Ghosts.. 55
Hand's-breadth 56
How a Stone Melts 57
Love.. 58
Closer than Breathing.. 59
Things I Never Said 60
Epilogue 61

The Stone Messenger

*Those who are willing to be vulnerable
move among mysteries —*
                                Theodore Roethke

This is how it was

You told me your name
I told you mine
we touched hands
and everything else
is just rain
or the spaces between rain
how we measured
seasons by angles
how we talked
like pebbles in motion
how we smelled
of the sea and each other
and how in the night
that was quiet with blue
or the memory of blue
you promised me sky
nothing more, nothing less.

Navigate by Moonlight

It was the night you took me moth watching
    the sky shaped itself around us
and breathing
    was a secret shared

You brought a picnic
    food and wine under shadowed cloud
among leaves
    never tasted better

Words flickered
    Cinnabar, Scalloped Oak, Garden Tiger
and an explanation
    of celestial navigation

No matter how hard we tried to hold them
    hours scattered
moths happened upon us circling silently
    leaving our dreams uncrushed.

For My Birthday

You gave me a stone, you said
it's shaped like a season, inside
I have placed a lost raindrop, our
first kiss, a broken guitar string
from when I tried to impress you,
your favourite poem by Yeats,
patterns of sunlight, a few
grains of sand and shifting
shades of blue. Each time
you hold it, you will smell the sea,
small wavelets will remind you
how we danced on an ocean
and the way summer falls –
lingers on skin.

Guilt is Quiet

Your glasses too big
for your face
teeth too long
for your mouth
in the first bed, left
of the door,
recognition instant,
you breathe my name
appear lost
in found sheets,
plumped pillows.
I said little
a lifetime exploded
in my lungs,
I did not know
this was the last time,
the last words.

Thinking of my Mother as Lauren Bacall

Perhaps it was 'The Look'
or how often you said
you loved Humphrey Bogart,
the pin-curled set, a hairstyle
that withstood winds on Dunoon Pier,
a daytrip with your friend Jenny,
fashioned in fur-trimmed camel coats
bringing Hollywood glamour
to an order of fish and chips.
Free to be post-war, out of uniform,
to be bold, lipsticked, to light
up a cigarette, laugh with young men
who thought they *were* Humphrey Bogart,
who dreamed of kissing you
in late night shop-front doorways,
sheltered from memories,
their bones grim, hollow
like mirroring ghosts
watching from windows,
while relentless stars
echo variations in time.

The Kindling

My mother is an installation artist,
an origami expert folding yesterday's
newspapers. She places them in the grate
swept clean of ash and cinder.
Dry sticks balance like acrobats,
shiny coal nuggets
take centre stage.
Later father will return
from work, fetch the toasting fork.
The room will fill with scents,
with laughter and family, each
of us unaware of what is to come,
how wind quickens
and mother sits alone listening
to the rain.

Looking at Jane Morris

I have no blue silk dress
no figure or face to tempt an artist,
there is no photograph of me
at birth, none with my father
an Enniskillen man, post war master butcher
whose hands boned and dressed dead flesh
planted choruses of daffodils
to chant their cosmic mantra
scooped an impatient daughter
onto his knee, slowing time
hiding an open wound. At six
a funeral is putting on
your best clothes
Hail Marys
watching the door.

The way I learned to tell the time

After school, climbing on to your bed
holding the small mantelpiece clock
with its reassuring tick, cuddling up
to wasting muscles, thinning bones.
You pointed to twelve, three, six
and nine, I learned of halves and quarters
to and past. Everything measured, medication,
meals, a daughter's repetition, and you –
horologist, amateur astronomer, tidal
locked, seeking the far side of the moon.

The Master Butcher

My father's back
began to crumble
during the Elvis years

he and my mother met
in the middle of the war
and married before the last
bullet was fired.

My father had been a gunner
and kept perfect time
on the dance floor
or playing the spoons

he could magic a sixpence
from behind your ear
or hoist dead cows
onto hooks to freezer-hang.

Summer 1959 he took to his bed,
no longer able
to shoulder the burden
of work or family.

January 1960 we followed the coffin,
widow and daughter,
lives hung as shadows
on a white horizon.

Winter 1960

My father is dead.
I do not know what dead means
and lie on the carpet
in front of a coal fire
in my aunt's house
playing marbles with my cousins
unaware my mother has worn
the same clothes for three days
has eaten nothing more
than a slice of toast, that grief
is swallowing her

I am firing my clambroth
my favourite marble
with equidistant shades
of pink, blue and green
certain I can beat the boys.
I shout *mum, mum look, keepsies*
my fists full of winning colours.
From faraway she stares, the dark
sockets of her eyes a twist of pain.

Leaving the Funeral Home in Enniskillen

My father's heart
cannot be found.
Its shadow can be seen
in the eyes of startled trout
released back into the River Erne
in the karst landscape at Cladagh Glen
in the polished creases of a Morris Minor
or nestled in grass
in his own back garden,
a child by its side
whose chatter pulses
to the beat of the land
where daisy-chaining
is the rhythm of life
communion of old ghosts.

My father's heart cannot be found
I hold it lightly in my palm.

January

Frost nips at our breaths,
this freeze-blast three days old,
the journey less than a half century
in the making, my mother
is widow-clad, her footsteps
make no sound.
Dogs have stayed at home,
traffic slows behind mourners
and the coffin carrying car.
On this street
of small childhood dreams
a priest recites the Sorrowful Mysteries,
head-bent voices thrum
on a silhouetted stretch of loss.

Blue Monday

Mother and me folding
and re-folding bed sheets
to put through a wringer,
the precision fascinates me.

Mother is strong, once
she wore a military uniform,
now widowed works two jobs,
but on Mondays is a magician.

The kitchen has a double sink,
six days of the week one side
is a work surface, uncovered
on wash day the magic begins.

I stand on a chair, rub clothes
against the washboard, colours
rosary around my fingers,
soap suds spiral and mother sings.

Walking Through the Door

I am greeted by shoes –
summer sandals, winter boots
fluffy slippers whispering
comfort. I remember

as a child
you would call out
'take off your shoes'
as the school day hung
itself in the hallway,
home-baking sweetening the air.

Opening cupboards and drawers
the years tumble backwards –
a butterfly brooch bought
for you in Edinburgh,
postcards from my European trips

and a black and white photograph
of you and dad in the country –
post-war picnic, borrowed car,
floral dress and open-necked shirt.
I can smell summer, taste
the brightness on your tongues.

Blue for Best

I am in my mother's house
the landscape familiar
past the Blessed Virgin
no reservoir of holy water
doors lead to ghost song
the close of blinds, a scent
of self that never left

On the coffee table
a month of dust, a mug
lies empty, I look for lipstick
stains, find your small make-up bag
tucked in the corner of a worn
armchair that fastened itself
to the turn of years

In the kitchen a radio
in the bedroom blue slippers
your favourite colour runs
through the wardrobe
giving life to the clothes
you kept for best but best is gone,
what remains is mine to fathom.

The Box at the bottom of the Wardrobe

An only child
it was always going to be mine.

Signpost to the past,
a wind blowing through leaves.

I trace a finger along birth,
marriage, death certificates,

names and memories smudged,
shadows in black and white.

A set of wooden rosary beads
twist around my wrist,

the crucifix hangs, a long-forgotten
prayer in this communion of lives.

This box, full of traps
and I gnaw at the bones.

Lowering the Coffin

As the cord slipped
through my fingers
I thought there would be
no tomorrow, no
more bluest blue skies
no more undressing
the heart, no more pleasure
of coffee and croissants,
the air breathless with
anger or pain or both falling
like summer rain, insistent,
uncontrollable, like a heart
that beats too fast then stops,
bones still jangling.

Handle with Care

They have not tasted blood
for years, wiped clean, polished,
on magnetic display, standing
to attention, awaiting your return.

You, Master Butcher, kitchen chef,
survivor of war, crushed and crumbled
from disease at forty five.

Your vegetarian daughter prefers
her knives smaller, concealed.
She packs another charity-shop box.
Pop of bubble wrap
punctures the silence.

Stele

When the stone is laid
I travel two hundred miles
to visit, quickly check
the wording is correct
then trace each letter
and number that represents
a second, a day, a year
in the lives of John and Mary.
Ignoring the weeping angels,
from my bag I remove a miniature
of whisky, take a sip, how you both
would have laughed to see this.
I pour the remainder over
the tendered grave, a pure
neat drop in the ocean.

Clearing the Path

All week, dreams
slipped the sheets
leaving me snow-bound
in a January fog

I have kissed my mother,
sewn a button on father's
worn work shirt and danced
the coastline of my lover's words

The stumble into New Year
leaves splinters of the old –
the need to break the skin
expose the pain that presses bone.

Coping Stones

If I whisper your name
no-one will hear
stone is the keeper
catcher of shadows

In my pocket
your last words
grey, unanswered
like rain from a slate sky

This dull ache
loss of colour
not even the blossom
can free me today.

Walking with Ghosts

They see me on my own
and think they will tag along
I am fine with it, really,
especially my parents.
Father no longer able
to hoist me onto his shoulder
content to stroll
and talk about the weather.
Mother looking like Lauren Bacall
tells me I can still be sexy at sixty.
Aunt Margaret bringing the family together
the crazy kitchen disasters,
I sympathise with each recipe gone wrong.
Friends come and go
as time allows, always busy
so much still to do,
offering opinions on everything
from the colour of my hair
to my love of chocolate cake.
These are the sounds
of my heart,
the keys that turn the locks
of passing years, the snatch
of voices on a path
in the quiet of my shadowland.

With a Feather in your Hat

You are studying lime trees
searching for the painless cut,
I am a passer-by looking up,
you say *it's time to prune*
I respond *so beautiful*
conversation is easy
and you tell me of your secret garden
a tree that can never
be felled, Jacobean, the cover
for two lovers, a marriage proposal
then war, she waited, he did not return.
I see a house, a Morris Minor parked out front
immediately tender to me,
like my father's heart
blowing on a Fermanagh wind,
my mother one step behind.

Thoughts of Spring

In the shadow of a wardrobe
hangs another life
a dress of summer purple
cotton, dune-creased, stroked

silver sandals beach-walked
revealing painted toe nails
glint of sand
tease of wave

somewhere I am that person
but not here,
here I am lost, city-frayed

counting stars
searching the breeze
my coat collar rippled
restless as thought.

Scotland to Sarajevo

I am sitting facing a wall
it is not unpleasant,
the wall is pink and behind the wall
I know Almir, whose flat we rent,
is tending to his produce
which he hopes to sell
at the local market

Beyond the pink wall
standing somewhere between
normality and uncertainty
the silent Igman mountain –
forever holding its wartime secrets
while karst springs produce
the water that I drink

Almir leans across the fence chatting
to his neighbour, I know little
of the language, I know *dobro*
means good, a useful word –
the weather is *dobro*
the food is *dobro*
the people are *dobro*

A helicopter overhead
in competition with
the muezzin's call to prayer
interrupts my thoughts,
there is little movement
except for a circling butterfly
escaping the shadows.

October sun is comforting,
today is *dobro*.

Mushrooms

Pretty umbrellas
or sustenance through war.
I am in Sarajevo
a tourist
in the rain –
late afternoon coffee shops
shuffle language and laughter,
I cannot write
about the mortar and bullet
scars on the buildings
across the street.
On my iPad I read
the siege lasted
one thousand four hundred
and twenty five days,
that mushrooms helped
starving families and soldiers
survive –
pretty umbrellas in the rain.

Sarajevo Springtime

Dandelion clocks message the air
and beyond the pink wall
voices are lifting away

Sun is high over the Igman Mountain
tractors plough
soil turns

Crows meddle
blossoms scatter
and it's easy to forget

Until my eyes drift, blink
at bullet-peppered walls
clusters of gravestones –

the backdrop to every season.

Sarajevo to Dubrovnik

Unintentionally we captured
a rainbow, the sky half dark
and the sun full of energy, mischievous
in an affectionate way. Perhaps
we had too many coffees or
the narrow roads and mountain
passes had raised our heartbeats
but here we are like go-betweens
carrying love letters or breathless
sighs from country to country
and this rainbow sneaking in
hitching a lift with no word
to the wind.

From the great book of distances

Donald tells me he is afraid
of leaving and having left
wakes in the night, thinking
of trees and roads and ghosts.
He wants to telephone, to know
we are ok but trees have no
numbers, roads are circular
and the ghosts do not reply.
So he gets up, puts the kettle on,
remembers Dan and his music,
wonders why the distance between
here and there is never less.

The Way of Tea

Donald lives in Edinburgh.
He owns two pairs of cowboy boots
and a collection of Patsy Cline albums
that he bought while browsing in charity shops.

Donald is a potter and a poet
he writes about train journeys
his American cousins and why he prefers
crows to people, their uncanny balancing act.

When we meet he says
let's go get some tea
tea cures everything
it stirs the bones

knocks down walls.
Donald tells me Samurai
warriors drank tea,
it's a spiritual experience

a slow stillness, the fragrance,
the naming of cups. Donald searches
for imperfections in the crockery saying
even the dead come back for tea.

Breaking Bread

My little brother does not
remember the names of his children.
He shuffles in slippers
from living room to kitchen
and looks around as though
in a foreign country.
I suggest we have sardines on toast
for lunch and wonder if
he still dreams of that big catch.
Fishing rods, a bicycle, three tool boxes
trapped in the garage, his son, Nicholas,
now drives the car.
Beyond the window, beyond the garden
a scarecrow stitched in the field.
Sometimes the wind here
takes everything with it –
a house that's lost its colours
its clatter of feet
its eager faces.

The Breathing Space

Your pockets are full
of vowels and consonants
words creased and folded
that wait like a jigsaw
puzzle to be smoothed
into sentences

But you are walking backwards
through closed doors, your timing
no longer exact
your mind-clock paused
with its hands adrift

I steer you to the garden
chair, with its cushioned covered
memories, familiar scents –
your wife, your daughter, your dog,
your eyes paint in abstract
like an artist inspired.

Finding Blue

The obituary reads
'wear blue'
soon I realise
I am *blueless*

Reaching for sky
I find only February grey
threads of cloud
and pale spit

I go to the sea
find the ocean swallowing
itself, spluttering
and coughing its tired mantra

In the high street
red sale signs
slope across
sleet-patterned glass

I walk like
a drunken ghost
in search of freedom
find only doors and walls

In the church winter sun
through stained glass
darts around shoulders
trailing murmurs of blue.

If We Choose To Speak

And if we could talk of the past
what language would we use
what maps, what roads
would take us
to where
we want to go

It's as if our tongues
are sewn up
our feet
steeped in a circle
and if the eyes
can't see it
the hands can't
touch it

So we settle
for silence
or the threat
of a storm
should a door
ever open
or close.

When I am Not

Waiting. There is a lot of that,
people with advice,
words to spare about rain
or the lack of rain.

I want the day to be beautiful,
cross out beautiful, overused.
I want this day to have meaning,
to have a smile,
a blue sky,
a bird in flight
or branch-tickling

I want to tell you what you already know,
that there is time, yet no time.
I want to know what the heart knows,
I want to know what crows know,
I want to know if my shadow
can take me back, not once but twice.

Over Time

I would always choose
the white pebble
seeing it as perfectly
unshadowed.
In my palm
it was weightless
an afterlife of loveliness
an unbroken seal.
At home
I placed it in a bowl
with the others
they rubbed along together
like skin and bone.

When Buttons Surprise

At a market stall
in Camden I'm turning
over buttons, boxes
and boxes of old and new

colours rounded, sized,
waiting to adorn
shirts, coats,
wedding dresses,
baby clothes

I remember at school
learning to sew,
hemming a square of cotton,
pricking a finger, drawing blood
to relieve the boredom

Years later, a summer's afternoon,
I repair your favourite shirt,
sew a few buttons that have worn loose,
you prepare a late lunch

Day lengthens
to meet the night in one long breath,
as buttons like moonsparks
fall to the floor.

In a World of Positives

We lived our life
in the rain
with the North wind
blowing in like
a fisherman's breath

It's hard to be carefree
with a river running
between us
with the smell of passion
continually washed away

So we become oystercatchers
take to shingle and rocky shorelines
we become noisy, joyous
sharing secrets
like some pretty sweethearts

Open-mouthed, laughing at rain
as it shapes itself
like silver arrows,
as it darts towards us
dazzling with attitude.

You Were Summer

I wonder how your world
has changed these twenty years
you the drifter
the weather gypsy

Staying long enough
to disturb the sea
to throw the runes
listening for an echo

I wonder if your
internal compass
senses rain
and turns away

Sometimes I think I hear
you circling the wind
but it's only a startle of leaves
in the path of winter.

After all this time

we do not talk of rain,
we sit at the cliff edge
with the sea lashing
and the years tumbling
backwards, air stinging
with promises not kept.
You repeat
we should stay here forever
the words are old
but still I want to wrap them up
carry them away with me
and on other days unwrap them
let them slip through my fingers
like glittering sand jewels
recently weathered.

Returning to where I've always been

It's not so much
that the scene has changed
the trees, the shop
the hill to the café
it's the same number of steps
going or coming
counting memories
your tallness in sunlight
or shadow, your laughter
unravelling like a slow addiction.
It's more
that the sweet air hurts
catches me unawares
turns me inside out
scatters fragments of days
and nights, of words
and heart. Nothing
prepares you for
not letting go

The Stone Messenger

Summer, outside the Nature Sanctuary
its roof stilled by heather, grass and moss

Inside the moon on stone floor
maps each journey

A warm breeze tracks the foxgloves
pulse of bees, dance of butterflies

Memories are folded into this building
meditation and songs, secrets of lovers

I stay for a while, listen,
the words keep coming back.

Findhorn holds my breath

I can smell wood smoke
on these final days of summer
sitting on a carved bench
like a detached ghost
staring at caravans
the Phoenix shop
the path that leads
to the beach.
Wind chimes
on trees
as shibboleths
signalling a way
through the past.

Blue Hour

It is an ordinary evening
a late sun dipping
an apostrophe of light
playing chase with waves
as I walk the shore road

In front of me your shadow
arms like melting stars
full of mysteries

You left with
the dandelion clocks,
for weeks I woke to the smell
of you gone, the earth spinning
its backscatter of love.

Seen in my everyday

I am no longer
that girl who named
trees, who walked
with you on the back shore,
who lay awake dreaming
of the space between
coming and going,
saying *here I am*
hearing *there you are*
so nothing was misunderstood.
And you gave me rain
and wild winters
a singing bowl
poems of Yeats
stones from your pockets
and the memory
of something
like wind
unseen
not captured.

How It Was

Some nights the air feels
warm around me
and the frayed ends
of an old day are mended

Unfinished jobs like weather
fasten themselves to morning
and I forget how years
have dulled

Listening to the hum of moon
I remember how it was to lie
dream-snared in dunes, love
threading its safety net of stars.

Resident Ghosts

The light, slant
through a window,
catches you slicing cheese,
wearing your black shirt
with its mad flowers
striking yellow,
summer resting in the bay
where earlier you'd swam
under a cloudless morning sky,
you can still taste salt on your tongue.
A girl crosses the room
smoothes a hand down your back,
she is threading time.
You continue to slice cheese
while outside the window
you watch yourself leave.

Hand's-breadth

I wonder which sea
borders your breath
or are you city-stooped
scratching for sky
tasting the blues
from your ocean walks, dreaming
of the space summer brings.
I try to picture your face, fragmented
I carry it with me
but I am no mime artist
cannot piece together the illusion
so I think of your hands
their pattern of veins
inking our past.

How a Stone Melts

Now when I dig in my pockets
there is only loose change
or worse a hole
where stars fall through

And if I think I can still
taste you, that last taste of summer
strung to my bones –
it hurriedly unfastens itself

My pain is ten years worn
ten years bled
I slip another stone into my heart –
stones were your talisman.

Love

Stones
        are warm
                under
summer feet
        and the breeze
                over
sand is how
        we speak
                there
is nothing
        but sea
                sky
everything
        we need
                gathered
scattered
        we follow
                stones.

Closer than Breathing

The mandala circle is eternity,
the centre my heart, a man
I have just met tells me this
on the bus to Findhorn.
I am having coffee with a friend
and he is going to a workshop
to paint mandalas. He says
we all have potential
we are all artists.
In the coffee shop
I repeat this to my friend
and we laugh.
Later I walk barefoot over pebbles
cross the sand to meet the waves –
northern cold, a sea-wind pinning
my heart to this place, to this shore
for eternity.

Things I Never Said

Today I walk
the Findhorn Road,
word-ghosts trip me up
cloud-fall trails
like an afterlife.
It could be Christmas
or Valentine's day
as I wrestle the wind
of old journeys.
This is the road of many
colours, of trees, bicycles
laughter and seascapes –
this is the last road I walk.

Epilogue

Always seeking the sea,
the breeze, the big skies
over the bay, scrying the
stones, searching
for home, sometimes
thinking I found it.

Indigo Dreams Publishing Ltd
24, Forest Houses
Cookworthy Moor
Halwill
Beaworthy
Devon
EX21 5UU
www.indigodreams.co.uk